Pocket Guide for the Most Awesome Fabulous Amazing
Volunteers and Program Aids a camp could ever be blessed with.

CONTENTS:

Graces

Games

Outdoor Cooking

GIRL SCOUTING: A W⊕rld of Friendship

GIRL SCOUTS

The Girl Scout Promise

On my honor I will try: to serve God, and my country,
to help people at all times and to live by the Girl Scout Law.

Girl Scout Law

I will do my best to be:
honest and fair
friendly and helpful
considerate and caring
courageous and strong, and
responsible for what I say and do,

and to
respect myself and others,
respect authority,
use resources wisely,
make the world a better place, and
be a sister to every Girl Scout.

Songs

Oh Ah Lay Lay
(Repeat After Me Song)
Chorus: Oh, Ah Lay Lay
Tumba tickie tumba
Mussa Mussa Mussa
Ah Lay Way, All lay way, Ah La Wha

It's Much to quiet,
We must sing it louder!
(Repeat Chorus until too loud – getting louder each verse)

Last Verse: It's much too Quiet, we must sing it quiet.

Announcement Song
Announcements, announcements, announcements!
A terrible death to die, a terrible death to die,
A terrible death to be talked to death – a terrible death to die!
Announcements, announcements, announcements!
Have you ever heard a windbag, a windbag, a windbag?
Have you ever heard a windbag, you'll hear one right now!

Grey Squirrel
Grey squirrel, grey squirrel
Shake your bushy tail
Grey squirrel, grey squirrel
Shake your bushy tail
Wrinkle up your little nose
Put it down between your toes
Grey squirrel, grey squirrel
Shake your bushy tail.

A Boom Chicka Boom

(a repeat song)
I said a boom-chicka-boom!
I said a boom-chicka-boom!
I said a boom-chicka-rocka-chicka-rocka-chicka-boom!
Uh huh!
Oh yea!
One more time…

Astronaut Style:
I said a Blast to the Moon
I said a blast me to the moon.
Blast me, Shoot Me, Blast me, shoot me, blast me to the moon.
Uh huh!
Oh yea!
One more time…

Janitor Style:
I said a Broom Sweep a broom
I said a Broom Sweep a broom
I said a broom-a-sweep-a-mop-a-sweep-a-mop-a-broom.
Uh huh!
Oh yea!
One More time… (Put next name of style here) style!

Styles:
Underwater: sing with fingers dribbling against your lips
Loud: as loud as you can!
Slowly: as slow and drawn out as possible
Opera: sing in an opera voice
Alien: high-pitched, beep sounds
Valley Girl: I said like Gag me with a spoon…
Mom: I said go clean your room
Dad: I said Go ask your Mom!

Black Socks

Black socks they never get dirty,
The longer you wear them, the blacker they get.
Sometimes, I think I should wash them,
But something inside me says oh no not yet, not yet, not yet.
Knee socks they never get higher,
The longer you wear them, the shorter they get.
Sometimes I think about anklets,
But something inside me says oh no not yet, not yet, not yet.
Girl Scouts they never get quieter,
The longer you know them, the louder they get.
Sometimes I think about muzzles,
But something inside me says oh no not yet, not yet, not yet.
(Variation: Substitute last line of every verse with: But something keeps telling me, no no not yet, not yet, not yet).

Bazooka Bubblegum
My Mom gave me a penny
so I could buy some tennies
but I didn't buy no tennies, I bought me some bubble gum
Chorus:
Bazooka zooka bubblegum,
Bazooka zooka bubblegum,
Bazooka zooka bubblegum,
My Mom gave me a nickel
so I could buy a pickle
but I didn't buy no pickle
I bought me some me bubblegum
~Chorus~
My Mom gave me a dime
she said go buy a lime
but I didn't buy no lime
I bought me some bubblegum.
~Chorus~
My Mom gave me a quarter
so I could buy some water
but I didn't buy no water
I bought me some bubblegum.
~Chorus~
My Mom gave me a dollar
so I could buy a collar
but I didn't buy no collar
I bought me some bubblegum.
~Chorus~
My Mom gave me a five
so I could stay alive
but I didn't stay alive
I choked on bubblegum.
~Chorus~
My Mom gave me a ten.
So I could live again
But I didn't live again
I bought me some bubblegum.

Little Red Wagon
You can't ride my little red wagon
the front wheels broken and the back wheels draggin'
slug slug slug slug slug.

Crocodile Song
Oh, she sailed away
On a bright and sunny day
On the back of a crocodile.
You see said she,
He's as tame as he can be,
I'll ride him down the Nile.
Well the crock winked his eye
As they waved them all goodbye,
Wearing a great big smile.
At the end of the ride
The lady was inside
And the smile was on the crocodile!

Moose Song
(a repeat song…repeat after every line)
There was a great big moose
Who like to drink a lot of juice.
There was a great big moose
Who like to drink a lot of juice.
Chorus:
Singin' way-oh-way-oh
Way oh way oh way oh way oh.
WAY oh WAY oh.
Way oh way oh way oh way oh.
The moose's name was Fred
He liked to drink his juice in bed.
The moose's name was Fred
He liked to drink his juice in bed.
~Chorus~
He drank his juice with care
But he spilled it in his hair.
He drank his juice with care
But he spilled it in his hair.
~Chorus~
There's a MOOOOOOSE
Full of JUUUUUUICE
On the LOOOOOOSE
(awkward pause)
~Chorus~

Jelly Fish
Wrists Together (repeat)
A jelly fish, a jelly fish, a jelly fish fish

Wrists together (repeat)
Elbows together (repeat)
A jelly fish, a jelly fish, a jelly fish fish

Wrists together (repeat)
Elbows together (repeat)
Knees together (repeat)
A jelly fish, a jelly fish, a jelly fish fish

Keep adding: feet apart, bum out, chin up, tongue out, turn in a circle

Forty Years on an Iceberg
Forty years on an iceberg
Across the ocean wide
Nothing to wear but pajamas
Nothing to do but slide (WHEE!)
The wind was rather chilly
The frost began to bite
Had to hug a polar bear to keep me warm at night
Tiddly om pom mm pom mm pom pom
Tiddly om pom mm pom mm pom pom

Here we sit
Here we sit, like birds in the wilderness
Birds in the wilderness. Birds in the wilderness.
Here we sit like birds in the wilderness
Waiting for _____ to come.

Princess Pat

The princess pat,
Lived in a tree,
She sailed across,
The seven Seas,
She sailed across,
The channel two,
And she took with her,
A rick-a-bamboo,
A rick-a-bamboo,

Now what is that?
Its something made,
By the princess pat,
Its red and gold,
And purple too,
Thats why its called,
A rick-a-bamboo,
A rick-a-bamboo,

Now Captain Jack,
Had a mighty fine crew
He sailed across,
The channel two,
But his ship sank,

And yours will too,
If you don't take,
A rick-a-bamboo
A rick-a-bamboo,

The Princess Pat,
saw Captain Jack.
She reeled him in,
and brought him back.
She saved his life,
and his crew's too,
And she did it all
with the rick-a-bamboo!
A rick-a-bamboo,

Now what is that?
Its something made,
By the princess pat,
Its red and gold,
And purple too,
Thats why its called,
A rick-a-bamboo,
A rick-a-bamboo,

Penguin Song

Penguins' attention! (What?)
Penguins begin! (Okay)
Right arm!
Have you ever seen a
penguin drinking tea?
Take a look at me, a penguin
you will see

Right arm
Left arm
Right leg
Left leg
Bob your head
Turn around
Stick out your tongue

Hermie the Wormie
Sitting on a fence post
Chewing on my bubblegum
Playing with my Yo-Yo (Woo Woo!)
And along came Hermie the Wormie and he was THIS big
(gets bigger with each verse)
I said, "Hermie! What happened?"
"I ate my mother"
Sitting on a fence post
Chewing on my bubblegum
Playing with my Yo-Yo (Woo Woo!)
And along came Hermie the Wormie and he was THIS big
I said, "Hermie! What happened?"
"I ate my father"
Sitting on a fence post
Chewing on my bubblegum
Playing with my Yo-Yo (Woo Woo!)
And along came Hermie the Wormie and he was THIS big
I said, "Hermie! What happened?"
"I ate my brother"
Sitting on a fence post
Chewing on my bubblegum
Playing with my Yo-Yo (Woo Woo!)
And along came Hermie the Wormie and he was THIS big
I said, "Hermie! What happened?""I ate my sister"
Sitting on a fence post
Chewing on my bubblegum
Playing with my Yo-Yo (Woo Woo!)
And along came Hermie the Wormie and he was THIS big (teeny
tiny)
I said, "Hermie! What happened?"
"I burped."

Pink Pajamas
I wear my pink pajamas in the summer when it's hot.
I wear my flannel nighties in the winter when it's not.
And sometimes in the springtime, and sometimes in the fall
I jump in bed with NOTHING ON AT ALL!
Glory, glory hallelujah,
Glory, glory what's it to ya
Balmy breezes runnin' through ya
With nothing on at all
NOT A STITCH

Tarzan

(a repeat song)
Tarzan
Swinging from a rubber band
Tarzan
crashed into a frying pan
Now Tarzan has a tan.
Tarzan
Swinging from a rubber band
Jane
Cruising in her jet plane
Crashed into a traffic lane
Now Jane has a pain
And Tarzan has a tan.
Cheetah
Gnawing on a banana
Cheetah
Slipped on a banana peel
Now Cheeta hurt his heel
Now Jane has a pain
And Tarzan s a pain.
Shamu
Swimming in the ocean blue
Shamu
Ran into a ski-doo
Now Shamu's gonna sue
Now Cheeta hurt his heal
Now Jane has a pain
Now Tarzan has a tan

King Tut
Doing the Egyptian Strutt
King Tut
Fell into a rut
Now Tut's on his butt
Now Shamu's gonna sue
Now Cheeta hurt his heal
Now Jane has a pain
Now Tarzan has a tan
Rhonda
Cruising in her Honda
Rhonda
Fell into her Ponda
Now Rhonda has no Honda.
Now Tut's on his butt
Now Shamu's gonna sue
Now Cheeta hurt his heal
Now Jane has a pain
Now Tarzan has a tan
Boy
Fell in love with Joy
Boy
Got beat up by Roy
Now Joy loves Roy.
Now Rhonda has no Honda.
Now Tut's on his butt
Now Shamu's gonna sue
Now Cheeta hurt his heal
Now Jane has a pain
Now Tarzan has a tan

Froggy Song

(Repeat song)
Dog!
Dog, Cat!!
Dog, cat, mouse!
Froggies!
Itsy bitsy, teeny weeny little yellow froggies
Jump, jump, jump, jump little froggies
Eating all the teeny weeny
worms and spiders
Bugs and fleas, scrumdidlyumptiou
Ribbit ribbit ribbit ribbit ribbit CROAK
(repeat again in a deep voice and
then again in a high voice)

Three Little Angels

Three little angels,
all dressed in white.
Tried to get to heaven,
on the end of a kite.
But the kite broke,
and down they all fell.
Instead of going to heaven,
they all went too…

Two little angels,
all dressed in white.
Tried to get to heaven,
on the end of a kite.
But the kite broke,
and down they all fell.
Instead of going to heaven,
they all went too…

One little angel,
all dressed in white.
Tried to get to heaven,
on the end of a kite.
But the kite broke,
and down they fell.
Instead of going to heaven,
they all went too…

Three little devils,
all dressed in red.
Tried to get to heaven on the
end of a thread.
But the thread broke
and down they all fell.
Instead of going to heaven,
they went to …

Two little devils,
all dressed in red.
Tried to get to heaven on the
end of a thread.
But the thread broke and
down they all fell.

Instead of going to heaven,
they went to …

One little devil,
all dressed in red.
Tried to get to heaven on the
end of a thread.
But the thread broke
and down they fell.
Instead of going to heaven,
they went to …

Three little Martians, all
dressed in green.
Tried to get to heaven
on a flying machine.
But the machine broke,
and down they all fell.
Instead of going to heaven,
they went to…

Two little Martians,
all dressed in green.
Tried to get to heaven
on a flying machine.
But the machine broke,
and down they all fell.
Instead of going to heaven,
they went to…

One little Martian,
all dressed in green.
Tried to get to heaven
on a flying machine.
But the machine broke,
and down they fell.
Instead of going to heaven,
they went to…

Don't get excited.
Don't lose your head.
Instead of going to heaven,
they all went to bed.

Llama Song

This is a repeat after me song!
And a do as I do song!
And a speak in a really funny accent song!
But first....We must summon the spirit of the llama.
LLAMA, LLAMA, LLAMA, LLAMA, LLAMA!
LLAMA, LLAMA, LLAMA, LLAMA, LLAMA!

I have a friend who is a llama
He wears a hat and coat
Do not take his hat and coat
'Cause it reeeally gets his goat!
  LLAMA, LLAMA, LLAMA, LLAMA, LLAMA!
LLAMA, LLAMA, LLAMA, LLAMA, LLAMA!

I have a friend who is a llama
He can really hock a loogie
You should see him a hock a loogie
While he shakes his llama booty
LLAMA, LLAMA, LLAMA, LLAMA, LLAMA!
LLAMA, LLAMA, LLAMA, LLAMA, LLAMA!

I have a friend who is a llama
He likes to sing and dance
You should see him sing and dance
In his llama dancing pants
Lets all do the llama dance
It is really quite a blast

Llama rock, llama rock, llama, llama rock
Llama shuffle, llama shuffle, llama, llama, llama shuffle
Llama twist, llama twist, llama, llama, llama twist.
Lllama Old School!

Watermelon Song

You can plant a watermelon over my grave
and let the juice (sssssipppp) slip through
You can put a watermelon over my grave and
that's all you have to do.
Girl Scout cookies taste so fine, but there's
nothing like a taste of a watermelon riiiiiiiiiiiiiiiiine
You can plant a watermelon over my grave
and let the juice (sssssipppp) slip through

Percy the Polar Bear

Way up in the land of ice and snow
Where the temperature drops to 40 below
Who's the happiest one I know?
Percy the pale-faced polar bear

Sleeps all day and then at night
Catches his fish by the pale moonlight
Has no worries, has no cares
Percy the pale-faced polar bear

Then one day a hunter came
Caught poor Percy by the snout
Put him in a great bug cage
Percy howled and he growled
But he couldn't get out!

Now he's living in a zoo
Funny thing is he likes that too
'Cause he met his girlfriend Sue
And she loves
Percy the pale-faced polar bear

Raptor song

Raptors one, raptors all; let's all do our raptor call.
Raptors one, raptors two; let's all tie our raptor shoes.
Raptors two, raptors three; let's all climb our raptor tree.
Raptors three, raptors four; let me hear you raptor rawr.
Raptors four, raptors five; let me do my raptor jive.
Raptors five, raptors six; listen to my raptor mix.
Raptors six, raptors seven; let us go to raptor heaven.
Raptors seven, raptors eight; let's go on a raptor date.
Raptors eight, raptors nine; let's get in to our raptor line.
Raptors nine, raptors ten; let's all eat our raptor friends.
Raptors one, raptors all; let's all do our raptor call.

Yogi Bear

I know someone you don't
know, Yogi, Yogi
I know someone you don't
know, Yogi, Yogi Bear
Yogi, Yogi Bear. Yogi, Yogi
Bear
I know someone you don't
know, Yogi. Yogi Bear.

Yogi has a little friend; Boo
Boo, Boo Boo.
Yogi has a little friend, Boo
Boo Bear,
Boo Boo Bear, Boo Boo Bear.
Yogi has a little friend, Boo
Boo Bear.
Yogi has a girlfriend, Cindy,
Cindy
Yogi has a girlfriend, Cindy,
Cindy Bear.
Cindy, Cindy Bear. Cindy,
Cindy Bear.

Yogi has a girlfriend, Cindy,
Cindy Bear.

Yogi has an enemy, Ranger,
Ranger.
Yogi has an enemy, Ranger,
Ranger Rick!
Ranger, Ranger Rick! Ranger,
Ranger, Rick!
Yogi has an enemy, Ranger
Ranger Rick!

They all live in Jellystone,
Jellystone. Jellystone.
They all live in Jellystone,
Jellystone National Park.
Jellystone National Park,
Jellystone National Park.
They all live in Jellystone,
Jellystone National Park.

Happy Llama
Happy Llama
Sad Llama
Silly Willy Nilly Llama
Super Llama
Mama Llama (Goose)

Happy Goose
Sad Goose
Silly Willy Nillly Goose
Super Goose
Mama Goose (Moose)

Repeat with following:
Moose, Mouse, Dog, Cat, Girl Scout

Old (new) McDonald

Old McDonald had a farm, e-i-e-i-o!
And on that farm he had a tree... (*switch tunes here*)
Where they cut down the old pine tree, TIMBER!
And hauled it away to the mill, tra, la, la!
Old McDonald had a farm, e-i-e-i-o!
And on that farm he had a home... (*switch tunes*)
Home, home on the range,
Where they cut down the old pine tree, TIMBER!
And hauled it away to the mill, tra, la, la!
Old McDonald had a farm, e-i-e-i-o!
And on that farm he had a dog, (*switch tunes*)
Oh where oh where has my little dog gone?
Oh where oh where can he be?
He's home, home on the range,
Where they cut down the old pine tree! TIMBER! and they hauled it away to the mill, tra, la, la!
Old McDonald had a farm, e-i-e-i-o!
And on that farm he had a Sweetheart...(*switch tunes*)
Let me call you sweetheart, I'm in love with you,
Let me hear you whisper,
Oh where oh where has my little dog gone,
Oh where oh where can he be?
He's home, home on the range,
Where they cut down the old pine tree, TIMBER! And they hauled it away to the mill, tra, la, la!
Old McDonald had a farm, e-i-e-i-o!
And on that farm he had a skunk hole... (*switch tunes*)
Welllll I stuck my head in a little skunk hole and the little skunk said to me...
Let me call you sweetheart, I'm in love with you,
Let me hear you whisper,
Oh where oh where has my little dog gone,
Oh where oh where can he be?
He's home, home on the range,
Where they cut down the old pine tree, TIMBER! And they hauled it away to the mill, tra, la, la!
Old McDonald had a farm, e-i-e-i-o!
And on his farm he had an ending. E-I-E-I-O!

Highland Goat
(Repeat after me song)
First verse – no parentheses
Second Verse – yodeling
Third Verse – fun phrases (in parentheses)

My highland goat (not a chicken but a goat)
Was feeling fine (had a glass of wine)
Ate all my shorts (red, white and blue)
Right off the line ('twas made of twine)
I took a stick (not a tree but a stick)
And gave a whack (smack, smack, smack, smack)
And tied him to (with a knot, not glue)
The railroad track (no time to pack)
The whistle blew (whooooooo)
The train grew nigh (it started to fly)
My highland goat (not a chicken but a goat)
Was sure to die. (goodbye, goodbye)
He gave a groan (ohhh)
Of mortal pain (Ohhh)
Coughed up my shorts (red, white & blue)
And flagged the train (this is the end)

e.

Go Banana's
Banana's of the world Unit!
Peel Banana, Peel Peel Banana
Peel Banana, Peel Peel Banana
Eat Banana, Eat Eat Banana
Eat Banana, Eat Eat Banana
Chew Banana, Chew Chew Banana
Chew Banana, Chew Chew Banana
Swallow Banana, Swallow Swallow banana
Swallow Banana, Swallow Swallow banana
Go Bananas. Go Go Bananas.
Go Bananas. Go Go Bananas.
Peel to the left, Peel to the right, Peel down the middle - Um
Take a bite

Romeo and Juliet
Romeo and Juliet on a balcony they met
Scram you guys, I got a date
Shakespeare's coming in 48

(Chorus)La-de-dah my sweet cream soda pop
La-de-dah, my sweet cream soda pop
La-de-dah, my sweet cream soda pop
La-de dah, La-de-dah, La-de-dah dah dah

Henry Ford was a grand old man
Had 4 wheels and an old tin can
Put them together and the darn thing ran
Henry Ford was a grand old man(Chorus)

Grandpa's beard is getting long,
getting longer day by day
Grandma chews it in her sleep,
because she thinks it shredded wheat. (Chorus)

I am just a little wild flower, getting wilder by the hour.
No one wants to sit next to me, cause I'm as wild as I can be.
(chorus)

Coca-cola came to town, Pepsi Cola shot it down
Dr. Pepper fixed him up, now we all drink 7-Up (Chorus)

7-Up got the flu, now we all drink Mountain dew.

Mountain dew got it too, now we don't know what to do. (Chorus)

Tiny Mouse
(Repeat after me song)
There was a tiny mouse
With tiny feet
Who sat upon
My toilet seat
So I pushed him in
And flushed him down
And that tiny mouse
Went round and round
And then the next day
He came back up
To seek revenge
(repeat again in a deep voice and then again in a high voice)

20

On My Honor

(Chorus)On my honor I will try
There's a duty to be done and I say "aye"
There's a reason here for a reason up above
My honor is to try and my duty is to love.

People don't need to know my name
If I do them harm then I'm to blame
If I help a friend than I've helped me
To open up my eye's to see
~Chorus~
I've tucked away a song or two
If you're feeling low there's one for you
If you need a friend, then I will come
And there's plenty more where I come from.
~Chorus~
Come with me where the fire burns bright
You can see even better by fire light.
You can learn even more by the campfire's glow
Than you can ever learn in a year or so.
~Chorus~
We've made a promise, we'll always keep
We'll pray so softly before we sleep
We'll be Girl Scouts together , and when we are gone
We'll be still trying and singing this song.
~Chorus~

Barges

Out if my window looking in the night, I can see the barges
flickering light; Silently flows the river to the sea,
and the barges do go silently.

(Chorus) Barges, I would like to go with you,
I would like to sail the ocean blue,
Barges, have you treasures in your hold,
do you fight with pirates, brave and bold?

Out of my window, looking in the night,
I can see the barges flickering light.
Starboard shines green and port is glowing red,
You can the barges far ahead.
(Repeat Chorus)

Make New Friends

Make new friends, but keep the old
One is silver, and the other gold.

A circle is round that has no end
That's how long I want to be your friend

I have a hand and you have another
Put them together and we'll have each other

Linger

Mmmm I want to linger, mmmm a little longer,
mmm a little longer here with you.

Mmmm it's such a special night,
mmm it doesn't seem quite right,
mmmm that this should be my last with you

Mmmm and come September,
mmmm I will remember,
our campin days and friendship true.

Mmmm and as the years go by,
mmmm I'll think of you and sigh,
mmmm this is goodnight and not goodbye.

Mmmm I want to linger,
mmmm a little longer,
mmm a little longer here with you.

I love the Mountains

I love the mounains, I love the rolling hills
I love the flowers, I love the daffodils
I love the fireside when all the lights are low
Boom-di-ya-da, boom-di-ya-da
Boom-di-ya-da, boom-di-ya-da
Boom-di-ya-da, boom-di-ya-da
Boom-di-ya-da, boom-di-ya-da

We Come from the Mountains
We come from the mountains, we come from the mountains
Go back to the mountains, turn the world around
We come from the mountains
Go back to the mountains, turn the world around

We come from the water, we come from the water
Go back to the water, turn the world around
We come from the water
Go back to the water, turn the world around

We come from the fire, we come from the fire
Go back to the fire, turn the world around
We come from the fire
Go back to the fire, turn the world around

We come from the sky, we come from the sky
Go back to the sky, turn the world around
We come from the sky
Go back to the sky, turn the world around

So we come from the mountains, we come from the water
Go back to the fire, turn the world around
We come from the sky
Go back to the sky, turn the world around
Go back to the sky, turn the world around
Go back to the sky, turn the world around
Yes go back to the sky...
turn the world around

Taps
Day is done.
Gone the Sun,
From the Lake
From the Hill
From the Sky,
All is well
Safely rest,
God is Nigh.

Graces

Addams Family
Du-nu-nu-nu (snap-snap)
Du-nu-nu-nu (snap-snap)
Du-nu-nu-nu, Du-nu-nu-nu
Du-nu-nu-nu (snap-snap)

We thank the Earth for giving
The food we need for living
So bless us while we eat it
Because we really need it.

Du-nu-nu-nu (snap-snap)
Du-nu-nu-nu (snap-snap)
Du-nu-nu-nu, Du-nu-nu-nu
Du-nu-nu-nu (snap-snap)

Alphabet Thanks
A B C D E F G
Thank you Earth for feeding me

Back of the Bread
The back of the bread is the flour
And back of the flour is the mill.
And the back of the mill is the wind and the rain
And the farmers will.

Cheerios
Cheerios, Cheerios
Every morning you greet me
Small and round, toasty brown
You look happy to see me.

Circle of oats may you sink and float
Sink and float forever
Cheerios, Cheerios
Bless my breakfast forever

Batman
Du-nu-nu-nu-nu-nu-nu-nu
Du-nu-nu-nu-nu-nu-nu-nu
Thank you!

Fork, Knife Spoon
Fork, Knife Spoon
Fork, Knife Spoon
Fork, Knife Spoon
Spatula, cha cha cha

Johnny Appleseed
Of the lords been good to me
And so I thank the lord.
For giving me, the things I need…
The sun, the rain and the apple seed.
The Lords been good to me.

'Neath These Tall Green Trees
"Neath these tall green trees we stand
Asking blessing from thy land
Thanks we give to skies above
For thy health and strength and love.

Superman
We thank the Lord for giving us food
We thank the Lord for giving us food
For the friends we meet
And the food we eat
We thank the Lord for giving us food

Peter Pan Thanks
(jump in the air, looking up with your hands on your hips)
Thanks!

Lollipop Grace
We thank the Lord for a hundred things
For the flowers that bloom and the birds that sing
For the sun that shines and the rain that drops
For ice cream and raisins and lollipops. (POP)

Games

Turn the Circle Inside Out

A circle is formed using all the players. Everyone joins hands and faces the middle of the circle. Everyone closes their eyes and tries to turn the circle inside out so that everyone is facing the opposite direction (outside of the circle) without letting go of each other's hands.

(Hint: the solution is that two people hold up their hands in a Y and everyone else follows though underneath.)

Back to Back

Players stand back to back with a partner with their elbows interlocked. Using each other's back fro support, the partners must try to sit on the floor and stretch out their legs. Then while keeping their elbows locked, the partners must now try to stand up without slipping or falling down! (Not as easy as it sounds)

Do this (and add something)

Form a line (or can be done in a circle). The first person performs a simple action, such as clapping their hands, touching their nose , stomping their foot, etc. After this, they turn say, "Do this and add something".

The next player repeats the first action and adds a new motion. (Simple motions are easiest). This sequence repeats all the way down the line or around the circle.

Version 1 – everyone does all the motions as it gets harder and harder.

Version 2 – If a player can't preform all the motions in order they go to the front of the line and becomes the first player in the next game.

Counting Game
Counting is a game that involves teamwork through looking and listening. Everyone stands in a circle, and the group must count to 10, in no pre-planned order. Only one person can speak at a time, and if two people speak at once the group must start over. This game can be adapted by using letters of the alphabet or, for an older group, the 50 states.

Group Knot
Group Knot is a physical icebreaker and could be done after a verbal ice breaker. According to Ultimate Camp Resource, everyone stands close to one another, placing their hands in the center. Next, everyone grabs another hand without seeing who the hand belongs to. Everyone must then untangle themselves without letting go of any hands.

Buddy Tag
Everyone gets into pairs, links arms, and spreads out. Then there is also a person who is the chaser / "it" and one person who is the runner. "It" tries to catch the runner. The runner can run to a pair of people and link arms with one person. There can never be a group of 3 people linking arms, so the person on the end of the pair then becomes the runner.

Bippity, Boppity, Boo
Form a circle and have a volunteer stand in the center. This person will point at another girl in the circle and say "(Name)". Bippity, Boppity, Boo!. The named girl must say the name of the girl in the center of the circle before she gets to "boo". If the girl in the center says "BBB!" before her name is said, she "wins" and returns to the outer circle. The girl she called on is then in the center and chooses someone new to "BBB!"

When they become comfortable with that level…add more levels along with "BBB!" Next levels have to be completed by 3 people in the by the count of 3.

Elephant: Center person uses their arms to make the trunks. Person to the left and right need to become the elephant ears.

Airplane: Center person drives the plane. Person to the left and right become the wings to the plane

Giraffes: Center Person places their hands directly over their head and together forming the neck. Those on the left and right arch their backs touching the middle persons toes to form the legs.

Quick Draw (Tarp Drop)
After participants have played initial name games, separate the group in half. Have two leaders / Pas hold up a tarp or sheet, then each group will send one member up. The goal is to say the name of the person on the other side of the sheet first. Count to 3 and drop the sheet. You can either just enjoy the game or keep score.

Group Juggle

Form a circle. Start by passing the ball to one person, saying her name, and instruct the group to continue passing the ball until everyone has received it once. Ask them to pass it again, without dropping it, in the same order. Let the group know they cannot change the order they are standing in, the order they pass the objects in or the challenge of keeping the objects from hitting the ground but they can change anything else. After having some fun adding in all the objects, stop the group and facilitate a discussion on what could be changed about their actions to make this more successful. (With younger scouts you can just keep passing the toys in different orders, focusing more on name learning and less on group problem solving.)

Maze of Life

You would need a grid area. This can be done with chalk and sidewalk, a tarp with duct tape. On a separate sheet of paper, draw the grid as it appears on your "Maze". On your paper (prepare for group arrives) draw a path going from a designated entrance to a designated exit. Participates can move forward and backward, side to side, but not diagonally.

When participants arrive: "Welcome to the Maze of Life, this is a silent activity during which your mouths are frozen shut so there is no verbal communication between participants. They may however use hand movements, and facial expressions. Explain directions of movement and the goal to get from the entrance to the exit if the maze. Let participants know how they will know if they are on the right path or if they hit a wall. I traditionally nod yes. And say BUZZZ if they hit a wall. Each person must make it through the maze once before the teammate can enter a second time.

Space Mission

Gather the team behind a start line. Scatter soft options or scrap paper on a flat, open surface. Explain one person will be blindfolder at a time and the team will use only their voices to direct their teammate to an identified goal, but the blindfolded person cannot touch any of the other objects along the way. Depending on age you can make the space larger or smaller, with more or less things to hit along the way. Have fun creating a story about the person being out in space avoiding aliens and rescuing the stuffed teddy bears, or whatever you will get your girls giggling or fits your theme.

Rainbow in a Bag

You: "When is the last time you saw a rainbow?"   Chat it up. Come up with a story about how you have a rainbow in your bag. Heckle them until you get someone vocal that doesn't believe you. Have that person come up to look in the bag BUT turn so that you block the groups view of the bag. Scream and blame the person for letting all the colors escape. Act it up a bit. Explain that the "footprints if the colors are left and get them to agree to help you to help you find all the colors again. Decide on a person to help see if they found the correct color. Hand each person a piece of a colored paint chip and have them look for that color in nature. You can break into teams to see who can do it faster. Or the team who finds the most colors for the rainbow.

Name Game

Make a circle with your group. The first girl or the Leader / PA will enter the middle of the circle by doing something silly and then saying her name loud and proud in the middle. And then returns to her place in the circle. The rest of the circle copies the person exactly. Continue to work around the circle until everyone has an opportunity to go into the middle of the circle. The sillier the better.

** Remember to challenge campers by choice. Let them do the game at their level of willingness to participate.

OUTDOOR COOKING

1 BRIQUETTE = 40 DEGREES

FULLY LIT

Preparing the Briquettes:
- ➢ Start charcoal 20-30 minutes before baking
- ➢ Fill charcoal chimney with paper and number of charcoal briquettes needed.
- ➢ Each briquettes = 40 degrees Fully Lit
- ➢ Read recipe for heat needed.
- ➢ When coals are fully gray, they are "ready"
- ➢ When using briquettes for foil cooking or Dutch oven you will need to occasionally tap the ash insulation off of them to help them to continue to radiate heat. Don't open a box oven just to do this, but if its open, tap the briquettes.

Box Ovens:

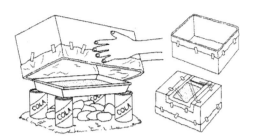

Supplies
- ✓ Cardboard box
- ✓ 4 pineapple / apple juice cans
- ✓ Aluminum Foil
- ✓ Cooking pan (9x13" or 8x8" aluminum pan)
- ✓ Charcoal pan – OR very thick aluminum foil
- ✓ Charcoal starting chimney
- ✓ Charcoal briquettes
- ✓ Paper / Fire Starter
- ✓ Matches / lighter
- ✓ Tongs
- ✓ Pot holders

Prepare your Briquettes (See previous section)

Lining the box
- ❖ Cut lengths of foil that are twice the height + twice the width of the box.
- ❖ Line inside of the box with foil, first from end to end, then side to side, overlapping foil and wrapping it around to the outside of the box.
- ❖ Can form foil over outside of box so it slides into the bottom of the box easily.
- ❖ The fewer creases in the foil, the better for reflection.
- ❖ You may use aluminum high heat tape to secure foil to the box and fill in any gaps.

Setting up the oven:
- ❖ Clear away brambles on ground so soil is clean. Never set up on wood or asphalt surfaces.
- ❖ Use foil or aluminum pan on the ground for base for the oven. (Shiny side up)

- ❖ Fill cans with water. They provide a moist even heat. Arrange them to support the corners of the baking pan,
- ❖ Find a rock to prop up the box edge about ½ inch for ventilation
- ❖ Spread hot briquettes with tongs in the charcoal pan / foil in the area between the juice cans.
- ❖ Place food filled baking pan on juice cans.
- ❖ Put the foil lined box upside down over the baking pan and hot charcoal, propping up one long edge with the rock, away from any wind blowing,
- ❖ Follow baking time directions for items baked.
- ❖ When checking for doneness, raise box slowly straight up (don't spill the heat), peek, then replace if more time is needed.
- ❖ Each time the box is lifted you will lose 25 degrees and will need to add 15 minutes of cooking time.

View from the top

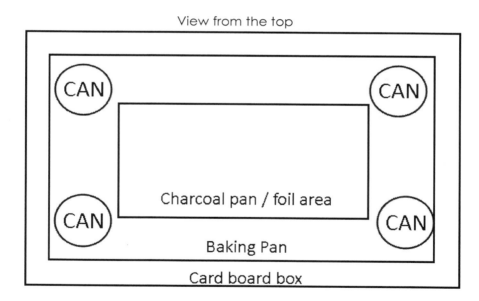

34

Foil Cooking

Supplies:
- ✓ Heavy Duty Aluminum Foil
- ✓ Charcoal Starting chimney
- ✓ Charcoal briquettes
- ✓ Paper / Fire Starters
- ✓ Matches / Lighter
- ✓ Tongs
- ✓ Potholders

Prepare your Briquettes (See previous section)

Wrapping your meal:
- ❖ Center ingredients on a 12x18" sheet of Heavy-Duty Aluminum Foil
- ❖ Bring up foil sides. Double fold the top.
- ❖ Label an edge to be folded with your name with a Sharpie.
- ❖ Double fold sides to seal packet, leaving room for heat circulation inside.

Cooking your meal:
- ❖ Using tongs, place your meal on the heated briquettes
- ❖ Halfway through cooking time, flip the meal packet using tongs

After cooking:
- ❖ Using oven gloves, Open end of foil packet first to allow steam to escape. Then open top of foil packet to cool and eat

Enjoy!

Dutch Oven Cooking

Supplies:
- ✓ Dutch oven
- ✓ Lid lifting Pliers
- ✓ Charcoal Chimney
- ✓ Charcoal briquettes
- ✓ Paper / Fire Starter
- ✓ Matcher / Lighter
- ✓ Tongs
- ✓ Potholders

Prepare your Briquettes (See previous section)

Cooking your meal:
- ❖ The number and placement of the coals on top of and under the oven is critical. The optimal number of coals used for any oven is based on its diameter. For example, if you are using a 12-inch oven you will need two coals per inch = a total of 24. More coals will likely burn your food and less may necessitate too long a cooking period. To determine how many coals go under and how many go on top, remember the magic number 2. Refer to following chart. Remember:
  - o 2 coals per inch of oven diameter
  - o Place 2 more coals than the oven size on lid
  - o And place 2 less than the oven size under it
- ❖ Using tongs, place the required number of briquettes on the pavers or cleared cooking order area under the oven
- ❖ Fill Dutch oven with the meal and cover with the lid
- ❖ Place Dutch oven on the briquettes
- ❖ Using tongs, place the required number of briquettes on the lid of the Dutch oven.

❖ Cook for the required time
❖ As coals begin to be ashy, tap on them to help them "glow" again. This removes the insulation layer of ash and helps coals radiate more heat.
❖ Using lid lifting pliers or heavy oven gloves, lift the lid and check on doneness.

Baking Temperature Chart

	325*F	350*F	375*F	400*F	425*F	450*F
8" Total Charcoal Top/Bottom	15 10/5	16 11/5	17 11/6	18 12/6	19 13/6	20 14/6
10" Total Charcoal Top / Bottom	19 13/6	21 14/7	23 16/7	25 17/8	27 18/9	29 19/10
12" Total Charcoal Top / Bottom	23 16/7	25 17/8	27 18/9	29 19/10	31 21/10	33 22/11
14" Total Charcoal Top / Bottom	30 20/10	32 21/11	34 22/12	36 24/12	38 25/13	40 26/14
16" Total Charcoal Top / Bottom	37 25/12	39 26/13	41 27/14	43 28/15	45 29/16	47 30/17

Fire Building

Elements of Fire:
Three elements must be present for a fire: Fuel, heat and oxygen.

Removing any element of the fire triangle prevents or extinguishes fires.

Fuel must be ignited before it will burn.

Burning will continue until:
- Fuel is cooled below ignition temperature
- Fuel is removed or completely burned
- Oxygen is removed or lowered

Three types of Campfires

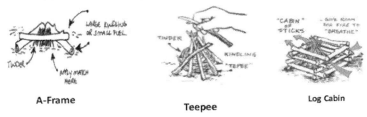

A-Frame

Teepee

Log Cabin

A) A Frame: Form the letter A with your Smaller dry wood. Place a fire starter in the middle of the A hole. Place small kindling on the Firestarter. This is a good fire for cooking and can be made in whatever size you need. It is also a good choice in windy situations.

B) TeePee: Take a small cone of kindling around a few handful of tinder. Once fire is going, you can begin to add larger logs in a standing formation much like a teepee. This fire is good for signal fires. It is good for directing heat upward.

C) Log Cabin: Place two larger pieces of firewood parallel with space in between them. Then add two more logs on top, perpendicular to the first set, making a square. Add tinder in the center of the square, adding a few more layers of logs, so that it starts to resemble a log cabin. Top off the square by adding tinder and kindling and now you're ready to light the fire. This is a good fire for cooking because it offers a platform for cooking.

For all fires… add additional kindling / fuel at the pace that the fire is growing. You want to feed the fire, but not cut off its oxygen supply. As the fire grows larger, the size of the fuel added can grow larger.

Building Fire Steps
1. Start by creating a safety circle. Remove flammable debris should be cleared 5 feet around the fire circle.
2. Use an already established fire pit whenever possible.
3. Have a water bucket full of water next to your firepit.
4. Make sure that loose clothing is removed and hair is tied back for added protection.
5. Have everything you need close by, you should never leave a fire unattended.
6. To start a fire, start with small dry wood and work up in size. Tinder – Kindling – fuel

How to start a lanyard

BASIC SQUARE STITCH

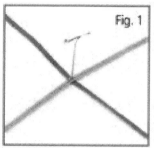

1. Secure lanyard in place with push pin or tack

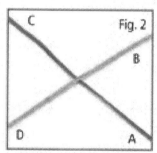

Use letters above as a guide

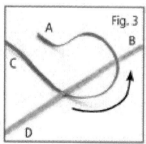

2. Fold "A" over lanyard "B-D"

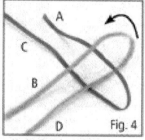

3. Fold "B" over "A"

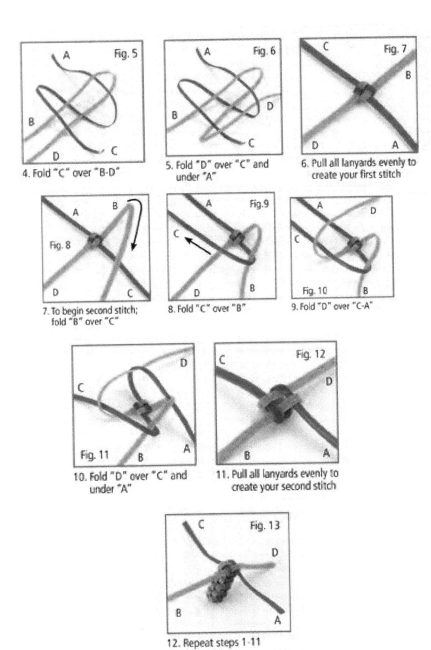

4. Fold "C" over "B-D"

5. Fold "D" over "C" and under "A"

6. Pull all lanyards evenly to create your first stitch

7. To begin second stitch; fold "B" over "C"

8. Fold "C" over "B"

9. Fold "D" over "C-A"

10. Fold "D" over "C" and under "A"

11. Pull all lanyards evenly to create your second stitch

12. Repeat steps 1-11

43

Flag Ceremony

Opening:
Girl Scouts, attention
Color Guard, attention
Color Guard, advance.
 Color guard will move forward in formation then unfold the flags out front
Color Guard, post your colors
 Color guard will attach flags to the pole and raise
Color Guard honor the flag of your country.
 Color guard will bow or salute the flag
Please join us in the Pledge of Allegiance
I pledge allegiance to the flag of the United Stated of America and to the Republic for which it stands, one nation under God indivisible with liberty and justice for all.
Please join us in the Girl Scout Promise
On my honor, I will try. To serve God and my country. To help people at all times, and to live by the Girl Scout Law.
Color Guard, dismissed.

Closing:
Girl Scouts, attention
Color Guard, attention
Color Guard, advance.
 Color guard will move forward in formation then unfold the flags out front
Color Guard honor the flag of your country.
 Color guard will bow or salute the flag
Color Guard, retire your colors
 Color guard will lower flag
Please join us in Singing Taps.
Day is done. Gone the Sun. From the lake, from the hills, from the sky. All is well, safely rest. God is nigh.
 (Color guard will properly fold flag in front of campers while taps is sung.)
Color Guard dismissed

Our Volunteers are the Best!

The traditional method of folding the flag is as follows:

(A) Straighten out the flag to full length and fold lengthwise once.

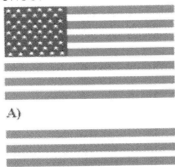

A)

(B) Fold it lengthwise a second time to meet the open edge, making sure that the union of stars on the blue field remains outward in full view. (A large flag may have to be folded lengthwise a third time.)

B)

(C) A triangular fold is then started by bringing the striped corner of the folded edge to the open edge.

C)

(D) The outer point is then turned inward, parallel with the open edge, to form a second triangle.

D)

(E) The diagonal or triangular folding is continued toward the blue union until the end is reached, with only the blue showing and the form being that of a cocked (three-corner) hat.

E)

Our Volunteers are the Best!

Day Camp Unit Volunteer Manifesto

I BELIEVE IN CAMP. I BELIEVE IN SHORTS, T-SHIRTS AND CLOSED TOED SHOES. I BELIEVE IN THE BUDDY LINE. I BELIEVE IN BUILDING STRONG INDEPENDANT WORLD CHANGING WOMEN. I BELIEVE IN SINGING EVERYWHERE I GO. I BELIEVE EVERYONE SHOULD KNOW 5 GAMES TO PLAY WITH NO EQUIPMENT. I BELIEVE THAT IF YOU PLAY WITH CHILDREN YOU WILL STAY CHILDLIKE. I BELIEVE CAMP MAKES A DIFFERENCE IN EVERY CAMPER LIFE AS WELL AS MY OWN. CAMP IS A PLACE THAT I CAN GET AWAY FROM THE RUSH OF EVERYDAY LIFE AND BACK TO THE BASICS. I COME TO CAMP FOR THE CAMPERS, BUT ALSO FOR MYSELF.

EVERY CAMPER IS AN INDIVIDUAL AND I NEED TO TREAT THEM AS SUCH. ONE METHOD DOES NOT WORK WITH ALL CAMPERS. I WILL STRIVE TO FIND THE BALANCE THAT WILL HELP ME SEE THE CAMPER AS AN INDIVIDUAL. AND HELP ME TO GIVE THEM A WEEK OF CAMP THAT THEY WILL NOT FORGET. I WILL REMEMBER MY FAVORITE CAMP COUNSELLORS AND TEACHERS. BY REMEMBERING I WILL DRAW ON THE POSITIVES OF THESE PEOPLE TO MAKE MY SELF A BETTER VOLUNTEER. I AM THE MOST IMPORTANT PERSON AT CAMP TO MY UNIT. MY CAMPERS WILL WATCH EVERYTHING THAT I DO AND SAY THIS WEEK. SO I WANT TO DO WHAT ITS RIGHT AND SAY WHAT IS GOOD. CAMPER SEE, CAMPER DO. I NEED HELP AND I WILL NOT BE AFRAID TO ASK FOR IT. THE STAFF WANT ME TO SUCCEED AND WILL HELP ME TO DO SO, BUT ONLY IF I ASK. CAMP IS CAMP BECAUSE OF THE PEOPLE THAT ARE THERE. CAMP IS GOOD, NO CAMP IS GREAT. IN FACT, I BELIEVE CAMP IS THE BEST PLACE TO BE. I BELIEVE THAT THIS IS GOING TO BE THE BEST WEEK OF CAMP YET. I BELIEVE THERE IS NOWHERE ELSE I WOULD RATHER BE.

I BELIEVE ITS ALL ABOUT THE CAMPER.

I am a Summer Day Camp Volunteer.

Our Volunteers are the Best!

To every Volunteer and Program Aid
that makes a difference
for the girls

Thank You!

You make a difference!

Disclaimer: These songs, games and information have been collected through other scout leaders, WDC, and from fellow Camp Oh Ah Lay Lay staff. We did our best to repersent the way that we do it at Camp Oh Ah Lay Lay. Thank you.

Our Volunteers are the Best!

Things I want to remember:

Our Volunteers are the Best!

Our Volunteers are the Best!

Camp Oh Ah Lay Lay

Made in the USA
Middletown, DE
31 July 2022

70268327R00033